W9-DCM-159

# Let Your Light Shine

## RAISING AWARENESS ABOUT YOUR CHURCH

Edited by James H. Heine

SAINT LOUIS

## Contributors

David Eberhard

Keven D. Ficken

Ronald Glusenkamp

Jeffery S. Schubert

Mark Schulz

Gregory J. Uthus

Carol M. Zemke

All Scripture quotations, unless otherwise indicated, are taken from the HOLY BIBLE, NEW INTERNATIONAL VERSION®. NIV®. Copyright © 1973, 1978, 1984 by International Bible Society. Used by permission of Zondervan Publishing House. All rights reserved.

Scripture quotations marked NRSV are from the New Revised Standard Version of the Bible, copyright © 1989. Used by permission.

Copyright © 1999 Concordia Publishing House
3558 S. Jefferson Avenue, St. Louis, MO 63118-3968
Manufactured in the United States of America

All rights reserved. No part of this publication may be reproduced, stored in a retrieval system, or transmitted, in any form or by any means, electronic, mechanical, photocopying, recording, or otherwise, without the prior written permission of Concordia Publishing House.

### Library of Congress Cataloging-in-Publication Data

Let your light shine  :  raising awareness about
your  church  /  edited by James H. Heine.
p.  cm.
ISBN 0-570-03750-8
1. Church publicity.  I. Heine, James H.
BV653.L49   1999
254'.4—dc21                         99–14397

1  2  3  4  5  6  7  8  9  10    08  07  06  05  04  03  02  01  00  99

# Contents

# Preface

West Coast. East Coast. Bicoastal.

Modern. Postmodern. (Whatever happened to traditional?)

Cable TV. Satellite TV. HDTV. The Internet, chat rooms, and e-mail.

Beepers. Digital telephones.

Satellites to help you plant your crops.

Commuter marriages, serial marriages, blended families, and soccer moms.

Main Streets. Mean streets!

Wow!

Whatever happened to Andy, Opie, Aunt Bea, and Mayberry? Whatever happened to the secure, predictable, we-go-to-church-on-Sunday world painted by Norman Rockwell?

It's all washed away in a deluge of the here and now, in a flood of images and information and new cultural norms.

There is no doubt that, at the cusp of the 21st century, we are living in a pluralistic society—and living in it, it seems, at warp speed. The world and all its people and cultures stand at our door, if not literally, then most certainly through the technological revolution we have witnessed in the mass media and personal communications during the last quarter of the 20th century.

There is no doubt, too, that this social and technological revolution has affected our families and the church. No longer do Mom and Dad live three blocks away or three miles down the road, ready to help on short notice. Uncle Tim and Aunt Jean no longer run the neighborhood grocery store or farm the quarter section at the crossroads, either.

In fact, Mom and Dad may be divorced, and we may live half a continent away from them. Uncle Tim may be in India this month, supervising a computer system installation. Aunt Jean may be home through the end of the year, then off to a university in Madrid for a semester-long teaching assignment.

Sound familiar?

Admittedly, your situation may be a little more domestic (if one can employ that word in a positive, non-pejorative sense), but in your own life there is your job and your spouse's job. There are soccer, dance, Boy Scouts, Wednesday evening's church council meeting, Thursday's parent-teacher conferences, a Little League fund-raiser on Saturday, and a family obligation Sunday afternoon.

And what about your church—your congregation?

No longer is your congregation the center of neighborhood life as well as a house of worship. For much of your "neighborhood," in fact, your church may be little more than an afterthought, a landmark your neighbors pass regularly. Sadly, it has little additional relevance in their lives.

In fact, if we accept survey results as generally accurate, out of all the families in your neighborhood, yours may be one of the few that has a regular church home.

As we said before, *Wow! What a revolution!*

This is a booklet about using part of that revolution, the revolution in mass media and personal communications, to reach out to your neighbors with the Good News of Jesus Christ. In a broad sense, this booklet is about evangelism with a lowercase *e*. It is about stewardship and servanthood, too, because through these same technologies you can help build up and sustain your community of faith.

In this booklet you will find firsthand accounts of what church professionals, their staffs, and their congregations have done to raise awareness in their respective communities about their church. This may be through redefining the role of the congregation in the community, developing a strategy to enhance visibility through local media, venturing into cyberspace, incorporating new technology into the life of the parish, or simply using the familiar church sign to offer passers-by an opportunity to smile and to wonder about the Christian community that gathers in the building associated with the sign.

None of these strategies are comprehensive; nor are the assessments exhaustive. They are provided in the hope that they will serve as a springboard for your personal reflection, assessment, and action.

As Jeffery Schubert notes in the introduction that follows, every Christian has been given unique talents—and every congregation has been "planted" by our Lord and Savior in its own unique garden—so we may serve and minister to the people in our community.

The technological and mass communications revolution of the past two decades has altered the way we live and relate to one another, to our church, and to our communities. As that revolution has swept away old ways of doing business, so also has it created new opportunities for reaching out to our brothers and sisters with the Good News of Jesus Christ, our Savior. We can let our light shine in new and different ways.

*The Publisher*

# Introduction: Bloom Where You Are Planted

*Know Your Congregation and Your Community*

*Jeffery S. Schubert*

As church leaders we are aware that people's lives have changed dramatically over the past few decades. We also are aware that their attitudes toward the church have changed.

People, church professionals included, appear to have less time now than ever before—despite all the advances in technology that ostensibly have made more time available to us. With working Dads *and* Moms now the norm, with all the extracurricular activities available for children, and with the increased pressure on those in school, just to highlight a few items, we seem to have less time now than ever.

Modern families are deluged by information—by newspapers and magazines and reports; by junk mail; by the incessant chatter of buy, buy, buy that bombards the senses from radio and TV, from telephone solicitations, and even from the Internet. (The noise of commerce, one could contend, forms the backdrop of our lives, compounded by the proverbial information glut.)

To counteract this, families have become more selective as to what they read, view, or listen to. (I suspect many families simply forgo reading books.) Many families are simply too busy to be aware of what's streaming across their TV screens or kitchen tables. Often, especially with printed material, they simply deep-six a lot of stuff, including information from the church.

We also are aware that there is more marital strife and divorce today. There are more serial marriages, blended families, and single-parent households than a generation or two ago.

All this has a bearing on the way a congregation communicates with its members and on the way it reaches out to its neighborhood and community.

## The Church and Its Role in Society

Regarding society as a whole, many people ask this question: Is the church relevant to me, to my family, and to this society on the eve of the 21st century? It sometimes seems that few give an affirmative answer to that question.

Often you hear people say, "I'm regular in my church attendance," but "regular" is not every Sunday. "Regular" means Christmas and Easter or perhaps once a month. So the Golden Age of Families—if there ever was such a thing—in regard to involvement with the church seems to have been years ago. Today it's an entirely different situation. We have to do business differently with the families and communities we serve when compared to the way we did things before.

The attitudes of people toward the church have changed in other ways too. First, denominational loyalty is not the same as it was in our grandparents' day or even in our parents' day. No longer are you Catholic or Baptist or Presbyterian or Lutheran because your family or even your community has worshiped in that confession for generations. Now the focus is not tradition or confession, it's utility. If families feel their needs aren't being met by your congregation, they simply pull up stakes and migrate to a congregation they believe will meet those needs. Often the denominational affiliation of the new church home is immaterial. The questions are simple: What's in it for me? What does this congregation offer to my family?

As church leaders we cringe at this caricature. We hope that our members, or potential members, ask more revealing questions, such as, "What does this congregation confess in regard to its doctrinal beliefs?" But the reality is otherwise. For many families in the pew, it's simply an issue of finding a congregation that meets *their* needs, whether those needs are worship style or education for their children or a support structure for their family.

I think we often practice a kind of herd mentality in the church. We see a particular congregation in a particular part of the country doing a great job with its constituency, and because that congregation is experiencing success, at least as we define earthly success, we rush to imitate exactly what that group is doing. When we don't get the same results, we wonder why.

Perhaps what we fail to consider is that the community in which our Lord and Savior has "planted" us is unique—just as the community of our model church is unique. Our garden—our community—should influence how we conduct our business.

So I suggest a simple approach: *Bloom where you are planted!*

## Know Your Congregation—and Your "Garden"

The first step? Know your congregation. Make sure you and the rest of your congregation's leadership understand what types of families you have (single-parent, blended, traditional, nuclear, etc.), the age groupings your members fall into, the health of your members, where your members live, and so on. Know your own congregation first. Know it well.

Second, and just as important, know your community. There are plenty of places to obtain demographic information, including, in my own denomination from the Lutheran Church Extension Fund. If you are a member of a different denomination, you probably have a similar resource. For a minor fee, you can obtain all the information you need.

Once you know the makeup of your community, you can begin to use that information to devise a ministry plan for reaching your community for Christ. This applies across the board, regardless of a congregation's circumstance. Every congregation has to tailor its approach to its particular situation. This is true whether the topic of discussion is the overall plan of ministry or the media or community relations or the evangelism component of that program.

This need for a tailored approach highlights one historic criticism of national church organizations—and even of publishing houses. These groups often have been accused of offering generic, one-size-fits-all programs, whereas, in reality, an urban congregation in a central city location will face far different challenges than a suburban congregation on the fringe of that same metropolitan area. The challenges of a rural congregation in western Iowa, Nebraska, or the Dakotas will be different from the first two as well.

It's appropriate at this point to remember Paul's words from 1 Corinthians 12: Every Christian in the church has been given certain talents, gifts, and abilities from the Lord, and everyone in the church needs one another to function as the full body of Christ.

I believe this analogy can be extended to individual congregations. We have different congregations called to serve different communities for Christ. Each congregation has its particular talents, personality, and characteristics so each can be a servant to its community. I believe that God has placed these congregations into specific geographical contexts to perform ministry right where they're at.

## New Flowers in a New Garden

Sometimes, of course, a community around a congregation will change. Then it behooves the congregation to call on the

Lord to give it the gifts to bloom in a new garden, even though it is a far different garden than it was 25 or 30 years ago.

What a congregation needs to do then, using the demographic tools mentioned earlier, is to understand the context of its new ministry. The members really need, out of love for their brothers and sisters, to learn as much as they can about the garden that they're now in, and then to see what God has given them as His people in that place to minister to their community.

Of this we can be certain: If God has allowed our church to remain in our community, we can be full of faith that God will give us what we need to reach out to our new neighbors and friends.

Sometimes, of course, that's where our own sinfulness intervenes. We say, "I know what I like and want" rather than ask, "What is good for this community? What will benefit my brothers and sisters?" It's at times such as these that we need to pray for the strength to subsume our own desires under the needs of those with whom we hope to share the Gospel. We have to love our community enough that everything we do will be for our neighbor's benefit.

## Cultivate a Sense of Mission

Often we get so hung up with the day-to-day business of running our ecclesiastical operation—paying the mortgage, maintaining the physical plant, resolving constitutional and bylaw matters, following procedure, and having meetings—that we nearly forget our primary mission is to seek and to save the lost and there are people who are going to hell because they are not in a right relationship with God through faith in Christ.

Sometimes churches have a "build it and they will come" attitude: *If* we add a family center, *if* we enlarge the narthex, *if* we … These churches get so busy, and sometimes so far in debt and strife over running the business of the church, that they forget the business they're in.

As people of the family of God, we need to remember our mission. Sometimes we need to reclaim our vision and our purpose for being, which is to find the lost. We also need to understand how to translate our mission and our vision into the actions necessary to accomplish it. This is not always easy, but it is necessary.

If we are to honor God and serve His people, we need to establish a blueprint for our ministry: This is what we want to accomplish. Here are the projects, the objectives, the activities. Here's the *who, what, where, when,* and *how* to get this done.

## Taking Minutes as the Hours Pass

The key is, of course, to keep things manageable. Break any plan into small pieces. If you give a member, or a group of members, too much to do, it becomes so overwhelming that no one can get anything done. But if you break the work into small pieces and employ members of the congregation that haven't been called on before, you can extend the work to more people, each of whom does just a small thing, which adds up to larger things.

A word of advice: Do not make people sit through meetings. Today, members are far too busy to sit through a two- or three-hour meeting once or twice a month to accomplish nothing more than taking minutes as the hours pass. Instead, say, "Sam, we're not going to have a lot of meetings, but we'd like you to address these 50 envelopes and mail them." This is something Sam will most likely be happy to do.

## Eternal Destinies

The chapters that follow focus on various strategies to expand your congregation's visibility in—and message to—your community, whether through local media, auxiliary programs, or a Web site. The essential cornerstone in all these efforts is that you first must know your mission and your community—and even your own congregation. You need to have your target clearly in sight, and you need to love your community and those who comprise your community. Without that commitment, we as a Christian family simply go through the motions. We have lots of well-run meetings and talk nice talk, but our hearts aren't really in the effort.

Sometimes in the rush of life we forget that what we are really talking about is the eternal destinies of our friends and neighbors and sometimes even members of our own families. If we take seriously the words of Jesus that "I am the way and the truth and the life. No one comes to the Father except through Me," that's pretty exclusive. And if that's the case, as we believe it to be, then the people we are trying to reach are drifting toward an eternal tragedy that is far worse than any temporal misfortune they might encounter. That should be a wake-up call for all of us.

The fields—our field, our garden—are indeed ripe for harvest. The good news, as we know, is that we do not labor alone or in vain. We have our Master's promise, "I am with you always, to the very end of the age."

Rev. Jeffery S. Schubert is the director of the Department of Family Ministry of The Lutheran Church—Missouri Synod's Board for Congregational Services. Rev. Schubert previously served the South Wisconsin District as administrative assistant to the District president, Youth and Family Ministry, and as District communications director. He has served parishes in Wisconsin and Nebraska.

# Using Technology to Integrate Faith with Life

*Gregory J. Uthus*

Integrating the Christian faith into the lives of the faithful always has been a goal of the church. In every age, part of that process for the church has been to employ the current technology to do two things: strengthen and sustain the family of God and communicate effectively the good news of Jesus Christ.

By today's standards, the "technology" available to the early church was rudimentary: paper and pen and personal testimony. To that, perhaps, could be added the Roman mail system, made possible by the roads Rome built. The Pax Romana ("Peace of Rome"), which made the roads and the mail system possible, provided the environment in which the apostles and evangelists could carry the Word to the far corners of the empire.

It wasn't until the 16th century that the church began to make widespread use of printed material, a development made possible by Gutenberg's work with movable type in the mid-15th century. In this century, of course, radio and television have come to play a part in the ministry of the church.

We have a stunning array of technology available to help us witness our faith to one another and to the world. From pen and paper and the printed word we have leapt, it seems in the blink of an eye, to personal computers, fax machines, e-mail, and the Internet, not to mention voice mail, digital telephones, and satellite TV.

If this chapter were to have a subtitle, an appropriate one might be "How to let your light shine in the suburbs, not only for your community, but for your parishioners as well." Not only has technology changed within our lifetimes, but so has the way we live. In this country, if not also in much of the modern world, a restless mobility seems to influence everything we do. People are no longer tied to family, church, or community in a way that was once common and accepted. Today, families may be separated by hundreds—even thousands—of miles. People marry and divorce. They move, then move again. It is in this environment that we as Christians live out our lives. Technology has accelerated the change we experience, but it also has given us new ways to communicate the good news of Jesus, to let our light shine.

## A New Revolution in Technology

It's fair to say that Johannes Gutenberg changed the world in the mid-15th century. Somewhere around 1446, after experimenting for a decade or so, Gutenberg devised a way to use movable type to print documents. No longer did one need to copy books by hand. Books could be reproduced efficiently and in great numbers using Gutenberg's new system.

We are, as noted already, in the midst of a similar revolution. It's perhaps a measure of how far we've come in this area that at the beginning of my ministry two decades ago, the most common communication devices in a church office were a telephone, a manual typewriter, and a mimeograph machine. My parish has the now-essential photocopier and fax machine, as well as desktop publishing-capable, networked computers with Internet access and e-mail. We even have a parish Web page. I do 80 percent of my personal and church correspondence by e-mail.

As a small suburban parish, we are probably typical in our use of technology. As individuals and adults we likely are typical, too, because we possess nowhere near the skill and savvy of our children when it comes to understanding this new flood of technology. (It's probably no surprise to you that our Web page was created by a young adult.)

17

This phenomenon has generated an interesting development. Young people are often more visually and orally oriented than their elders, not only because of computers, but also because of that other 20th-century product, the television set. In some respects we are moving beyond the written word, perhaps returning to a more visual, pre-Gutenberg culture.

Before Gutenberg made printing practical, the church taught its members in part through painting and sculpture. This is the way the laity processed theology and the reason the cathedrals of Europe are such great repositories of art. The majority of people could not read, and they learned the Christian faith through the spoken word and through the visual arts. After Gutenberg, the printed word gradually eclipsed this traditional means of communication.

In a sense we're taking a step backward, or perhaps rediscovering a lost sense of the visual as a learning tool. If you visit larger churches, you may see an increased use of painting and sculpture because we are finding again that people respond to visual cues.

All this is not entirely the result of computers, but they have opened new doors to visual communication, and they have opened new ways for congregations to communicate with their members and their communities.

## A Mission and a Vision

Before we proceed too far, I believe it's appropriate to reflect a little on our vision here at Trinity, on how we see ourselves as God's servants in this community.

As I noted earlier, we are a suburban congregation of about 200 families. We celebrated our half-century mark in 1997, and over the past few years we have experienced a slow, steady growth that adds about 10 or 12 families a year.

Our staff is small by many standards—a director of music, a director of youth and family, a church secretary, a part-time business manager, a part-time custodian, and myself as pastor. Internally, we have an in-house office system and computer network that allows us to manage the day-to-day business of the church in a relatively efficient manner. We have two Sunday morning services, a Sunday school, vacation Bible school in the summer, an August music camp, and the requisite roster of volunteer and auxiliary organizations.

Most of our members are working parents who juggle the standard repertoire of family issues: work, kids, the mortgage, stress, aging parents, church and community commitments, etc. We also have a large number of young members away at college, and from time to time, we have members who travel to the far corners of the earth for reasons of work or recreation.

Three years ago—though we actually began the process long before that—we put in place a vision of what we do as a congregation. Our vision statement, in a nutshell, is this: *Integrating Faith with Life.* The reason we say *faith with life* and not *life with faith* is that we believe everyone is at a different stage in their life in terms of their understanding of who God is and who they are and how all this fits together.

Our vision statement informs everything we do. It helps us keep our mission in focus. For a church to do well, I believe it needs to make a connection somehow for its members, and for its community, between what it believes and holds to be true and everyday life. It needs to demonstrate that its doctrines and beliefs actually influence the way people live.

This is our goal for Trinity—to make what we believe connect with our daily lives so faith is not something in our heads but actually a *life*style. Our hope is that we as members of the body of Christ begin to see that God does have an impact on our daily lives and that we in turn live out that message in our community.

## The Essentials

So what does this have to do with PCs and e-mail and Web access?

We use these tools—and that is what they are, tools—to help people make the connection between faith and life. We still have a way to go, of course, and not everything we have tried has been as fruitful as we had hoped, but we can offer this recipe for how to begin.

### Update and integrate your office equipment.

If you're a small church without a lot of money, begin with the basics: a PC with sufficient memory, a color printer, a scanner, desktop publishing capability, and access to the Internet. This and the photocopier and fax machine you probably have already will serve you well. From there, if you choose, you can move to laptops and programs that do visual multimedia processing, which can open a whole new world of possibilities.

### Create a Web page and expand your use of e-mail.

The former will provide a snapshot of your congregation for the whole world, and the latter can be an effective tool for maintaining a link with congregational members on the job away from home or students away at school. It also can provide an efficient means for boards and committees to conduct business without the necessity of meetings that can drone on endlessly or simply consume too much time. Not everything can be done by e-mail, but often a lot of routine business can be expedited through a judicious use of e-mail.

Your Web page also can serve as a handy reference tool. In addition to listing our location and principal church telephone number, we post a monthly calendar and various secondary telephone numbers and contacts. This information about the church and its leaders is readily accessible to members and nonmembers.

If your knowledge of Web skills is modest, your national denomination will most likely have someone who can help, or you may discover, as we did, that there is help right in your congregation.

## Move technology out of the office and into the classroom and the sanctuary.

Computers are not only great business machines, they can be great creative tools too. Recently, with the help of computer technology, I have begun to use multimedia aids in worship services. A forthcoming sabbatical will be devoted to improving my multimedia skills. My goal is to be able to use a laptop and a video projector effectively during the sermon or the liturgy.

A friend in Colorado has developed an excellent liturgical program. When the congregation begins to chant the liturgy, she displays pictures that illustrate the liturgy in sequence with the music. As a member of that congregation, you not only repeat words that are so familiar you can recite them in your sleep, you see visual representations of those words also. It's not a feature I would want to use every week, but from time to time it can be very effective.

The other opportunity to employ computer-generated graphics is in the classroom. I especially want to extend this kind of visual help to confirmation instruction. Thus when I'm teaching the catechism, and the children are studying the Ten Commandments or the Apostles' Creed, I can make it interesting and engaging for them.

## Employ your local media to raise awareness about your church.

This is not strictly a "technology" issue, but many things the media can do today are a direct result of the technological advances of the last quarter century. Elsewhere in this booklet Carol Zemke explains the ABCs of working with the media, especially local or community newspapers, which can be a great asset for establishing a congregation's presence in the community.

We also take advantage of the advertising opportunities offered by our local newspapers. We do not advertise with our metropolitan daily because its sweep is too broad for our "market" and for our resources. Through our community newspapers, we can direct our advertising to the one or two ZIP codes where it will have greatest impact.

What do we advertise? We limit our advertising to special events and services. For example, for the past several years I have incorporated chalk drawings into the Sunday services twice a year. We advertise those services because they have broad appeal. We advertise our August music and drama camp for the same reason.

Our music and drama camp has grown into a major community event. We estimate that 70 percent of the children who participate in the camp come from nonmember families. It has been such a success that we have a waiting list, and we're beginning to contemplate how we will handle the camp when it outgrows our facilities.

Advertising also has helped us establish our physical location in the community. Because we are on a neighborhood street away from a principal thoroughfare, we are hard to find, even for people who are familiar with the community. Once they find us, they like what they see, but until we began our advertising campaign, many people simply were not aware of us.

## A Brave New World

Generations ago, if your parents attended a particular church in a particular community, you went to that church and your kids probably went there too. Today, it's not unusual for people to attend two or three different churches within their lifetime. It's not unusual to switch denominations or drift in and out of regular church membership or attendance. Before, life was parochial: You stayed in one community and one congregation from the time you were baptized until the time you died. That seldom happens anymore.

As church leaders and as congregations we need to think about how we meet people's needs and how we can connect with them. Technology has changed the way we live; it also has provided new avenues for connecting with people. With a little thought, planning, and vision on our part, we can use that technology to reach people in our neighborhood, in our city, and around the world with the good news of Jesus. In other words, technology can be a great asset when seeking to integrate faith with life.

Rev. Gregory J. Uthus is pastor of Trinity Lutheran Church, Kirkwood, Mo. In addition to his master of divinity degree from Wartburg Theological Seminary, Rev. Uthus holds a bachelor's degree in art from California Lutheran College. Rev. Uthus employs his visual arts background in as many ways as possible in the proclamation and teaching of God's Word, including numerous commissions from religious organizations. In addition to Trinity, he has served parishes in Colorado and Kansas.

# The ABCs of Media Relations

*Carol M. Zemke*

It hasn't been easy for many congregations to feel comfortable using the media to publicize their activities. Historically, the trend in many churches has been to keep to themselves about events and activities. The annual children's Christmas program is a classic example of this tendency. Usually, invitations are sent home to the parents, and an announcement of the program appears in the church bulletin or newsletter, but no one sends an announcement to the local paper.

If you read your local newspaper and see a story about the neighborhood Methodist or Baptist or Episcopal church, you may conclude that they are active in the community and their events are significant. Because your church does not appear in the same pages, it's easy to assume that you are not active or significant.

This is a false assumption. The difference between you and the congregation in question may be that it employs an effective public relations strategy.

## Public Relations—Making Contact with the Media

It's smart to add a public relations committee or board to your church council, or at least to appoint someone to serve as PR director. He or she will be responsible for overseeing your church's media outreach.

Most likely, your congregation's PR director will be on a limited budget or on no budget at all. This doesn't mean that the pursuit of quality can't exist. Because much of your work will involve the written word, the following describes four ways you can pursue high PR quality on a low budget.

### Research

Emulate quality. Read widely. Study newspapers, magazines, advertising of all sorts, and newsletters. Evaluate style in writing, layout, and presentation. Take note of techniques that you can apply to your own work. Know the difference between good and bad writing. Use your library or search the Internet for material to help you learn more about great publications.

### Recruit

Evaluate your own talents and select people to fill in the gaps in your expertise. Writing tasks often can be delegated to others who know more about the subject to be publicized. *Use many people to proofread all work!* Asking another person to proofread a document before it's printed is a good quality-control check. An "outsider" may question the meaning of something because the subject is new to him or her. Recruit help from church members with computer, layout, and design skills.

### Reevaluate

Reread the materials you have produced over the years. Check to see if they are easy to read and attractive. Do the materials speak to the appropriate audience? Compare your work with the magazines, newsletters, and other publications you have studied. Work on improving the writing, the layout, and especially the printing and distribution of your material.

### Compile

Compile a list of words that describe your congregation. Use these words with all public relations material. These words should be descriptive of your congregation, and they must be honest. If your people are caring, and outreach is an easy thing for the members of your church, then describe yourself as a caring and evangelistic church.

Select a theme or slogan for the church year and use it throughout the year. Many denominations will select an annual theme. You may want to employ the same theme. This gives unity to all your church activities. Use the logo developed for the theme on your stationery as an additional way to enhance the work your church does. The logo can be used in worship bulletins and newsletters as well.

## Newspapers

The easiest coverage to garner is generally newspaper coverage. This is true because most newspapers are looking for good news. Therefore make your church news *good news.*

Tell it like it is. Promote your services and special events. Use pictures whenever possible. A picture with a good caption, as the old saying goes, "is worth a thousand words"! Tell the *who, what, where,* and *when* in every article you write.

The best way to obtain a reliable source of photos from your church activities is to assign someone to take the pictures. Be specific about the photos you want. Each photo sent to an editor should be accompanied by a caption that explains the picture. *Be sure to list all names and titles correctly!*

Photos should be vivid and bright. A close-up of people no more than four feet away is best for publication. For a group photo, use a wide-angle lens. Make photos interesting by having people do something natural instead of simply standing in a line.

One of the best ways to take good pictures is to take a lot of pictures. Then compare the shots and choose the best one for submission.

Get to know your local newspaper editor or the paper's religion editor if the publication is large and has numerous departments. Editors will come to depend on you if you send them good material on a routine basis. Occasionally, invite an editor to an activity to see firsthand the life of your church.

Small-town or community newspapers often give the best coverage. Plan ahead by scheduling sufficient time to meet deadlines. Gather all accurate and pertinent information before you start to write. Make your introduction lively to catch your reader's interest. In journalism, it's essential to establish the facts quickly, with the most important elements first. Keep your sentences short and to the point. Check and recheck the facts. Verify the spelling of names and the titles of people. Know your audience. Don't assume your readers are familiar with your church. Spell out full names and officers' titles. Let the readers know your church is alive and well. Make them want to attend your services and activities because your writing makes the experience sound worthwhile.

## Radio

Radio coverage can be hard to obtain unless you have a local station that devotes substantial time to promoting current events for local organizations. Small-town radio stations often help nonprofit organizations promote their events. Use this opportunity extensively. It may become your best means of advertisement. If you live in a large city with numerous radio stations, find a station with a religious format and send your material to it. Or you may find a station that likes to do free spots for nonprofit groups.

As with newspapers, send your articles and news items regularly. Know your station leaders. If there is a religion department and a person responsible for that department, send your material to that person by name and title. If appropriate, ask that person to speak at a church event, just to get to know him or her better.

## Television

Cable TV has opened new doors to the world of television for community organizations. Check with your local cable company to find out what their policy is on community access for churches and other religious organizations.

If you are able to obtain air time, be sure to take advantage of it, but first make sure you are ready to broadcast quality programs. Your cable company may loan you a camera for recording your service or special event. The company also may teach you how to edit the film properly and introduce you to other dos and don'ts. Each cable company has its own policy regarding these issues, but it's worth looking into because of the outreach opportunities cable television provides.

Elsewhere in this booklet, Mark Schulz explains how his congregation began its cable TV career. He offers an in-depth look at the benefits cable TV can offer.

## The Internet

Many congregations have members who are computer literate. You may even have programmers or analysts in your congregation who will volunteer their time to help your congregation become part of the electronic superhighway.

A Web site on the Internet can be used for many things. It can serve as a directory for someone visiting (or moving to) your town and looking for a church to attend. It can list all the activities of your congregation for a month or a particular season. For many congregations, a Web site can be more cost effective than traditional print or broadcast advertising.

As with cable TV, you will find an entire chapter in this booklet devoted to the Internet and the World Wide Web. Keven Ficken offers a sound introduction to this new technology.

## Church Signs

If your city or regional government allows you to erect a sign on your church property, take advantage of this excellent PR tool. If a lighted sign is permitted, go for it, and the larger the better, especially if you are adjacent to a busy highway or city street.

For a thorough discussion of the benefits you can derive from your church sign, see Ron Glusenkamp's chapter. After you read his chapter, you'll never think of your church sign in the same way again.

## Promote and Energize Publicity

The secret to a successful PR campaign is to energize the publicity. What's the best way to do this? *Prepare and plan ahead!* Promote meetings and activities months in advance. Put dates on your calendar. Make publicity personal. Make it an invitation, and tell your readers why they should attend. (Give a good reason. People are too busy to attend everything. They want to know what's in it for them.) Make the publicity eye-catching. Be unique. Use your imagination and creativity to get attention.

Plan different ways to promote the same event. Statistics show that it takes seven separate appearances for people to see something in print and remember it.

As mentioned earlier, it's important to use short, snappy sentences. But be informative. Make sure you make clear *who* is sponsoring the meeting, *who* is the speaker, and *who* is providing the entertainment. Make sure you explain *where* and *when* the event is being held and *what* the event is all about. Provide details about the event so everything is laid out for all to understand.

People need many reminders. Use the church newsletter and bulletin, news releases, posters and flyers, personal invitations, phone calls, the Internet, and cable TV to spread your message. Use them to energize your publicity.

## Plan, Plan, Plan

It's important to plan the whole year in advance with each committee or board of your church and to set up an annual calendar of events. This will make it easier to know when to publicize each event. Then it's important to create a timetable that shows when material should be prepared, mailed, or posted. This planning will also tell you how much help and support you will need.

Be the best you can be. Continually add new words that describe your church to your list. Your media coverage will depend on how organized you want to be. Never be afraid to get too much publicity out to the public or to your congregation.

## Sample Plan

- Meet with the committee in charge of the special activity. Include the pastor if necessary. Meet well in advance of the activity.

- Find out the exact plan for the activity. Make sure you have the correct date, time, place, and exactly what the activity is called and what it is all about. Know who is involved by name and title and what roles these individuals play.

- Find out if there is a color scheme. This will help if posters or flyers are going to be part of the publicity.

- Ask about the budget for publicity.

- Establish whether the event is open to the public or reserved for members of the congregation. This will tell you how to publicize the event.

- Make sure you know everything there is to know about the event. Repeat what you have learned back to the committee to confirm that you have the correct information.

Carol M. Zemke is chairman of the International Lutheran Women's Missionary League Public Relations Committee. She is also Director of Major Gifts for Trinity First Lutheran Church and School, Minneapolis, Minn. Ms. Zemke is a past director of public and church relations for Concordia University, St. Paul, Minn.

# Cathedral Ministries

*Staying Visible—and Viable—in an Urban Setting*

*David Eberhard*

As the landscape of America's urban centers has changed, so has the makeup and fortunes of its churches. Over the past two or three generations, many city churches have merged, moved to the suburbs, or closed and sold their property. Other congregations remain, sometimes shadows of their former selves, seeking to retain a tenuous grasp on their heritage and mission.

For some of these churches, especially those strategically located within urban cores, a cathedral ministry could be a step in the direction of assuring that a church presence will remain in the city.

My church, Historic Trinity Lutheran Church, Detroit, Mich., is one such church. Founded in 1850 as the first Lutheran Church—Missouri Synod parish in Detroit, it soon became the mother church of local Lutheran congregations. Historic Trinity gave birth to 13 mission congregations throughout the city, and those 13 congregations grew into 132 parishes.

Early in its history, Historic Trinity became the "Cathedral Church" for Lutherans in and around Detroit. At Trinity they gathered for special worship services and to organize such institutions as the Lutheran School for the Deaf, the nationwide radio capability of the "The Lutheran Hour," the Lutheran High School Association, and Valparaiso University.

Historic Trinity began in 1850 in a frame building on Larned Street. In 1866, just a year after the end of the Civil War, the congregation dedicated a red-brick church building on the parish's present site at Gratiot and Rivard. That structure was replaced in 1931 by our present Gothic-style building, which is reminiscent of the great urban cathedrals of Europe. Today Trinity is listed as an historic site on local, state, and national registers.

In keeping with our rich heritage, we offer worship services in the Lutheran liturgical tradition. We strive to provide the finest in preaching, teaching, and inspiring music. We also serve as a focal point for special worship services for individuals throughout the Detroit region.

By resolution of the Michigan District of The Lutheran Church—Missouri Synod and our congregation, Historic Trinity is the "seat" of the president of the Michigan District. District presidents use Historic Trinity as their home church in Detroit. The district president's chair, located in the chancel, is used by the president alone. Various boards and committees of the Michigan District frequently employ the facilities of Historic Trinity as well, as do many regional auxiliary groups.

## What Is a Cathedral Ministry?

A cathedral ministry emanates from a centrally located church building in a major city. The cathedral church becomes the focal point for its denomination in that region. It provides the site where joint activities, meetings, and special worship services take place. The cathedral church is often the seat of the denomination's presiding officer, whether bishop or president, and it traditionally includes a location for the burial of the faithful.

The parish of a cathedral ministry is metropolitan in outreach. It provides quality programs, employs staff sufficient to carry out its various ministries, and offers a wide variety of music and worship services. As the region's locus of denominational life, special worship services, civic religious activities, and the celebration of special feast days commonly take place within its sanctuary.

33

## Rooted in History and Service

A brief history of cathedral churches is appropriate at this point: In the 12th and 13th centuries, the cathedrals of Europe's great cities became the focus of urban life even as the cities themselves began to exert an influence over the surrounding regions. By becoming open and inclusive, these urban cathedrals reversed the inward-looking direction of monastic life. They combined the secular with the religious and became places in which the issues of life could be discussed and the solutions to problems debated. The religious life of a cathedral encompassed all living things, and its worship service was the center of all life.

Historically speaking, a cathedral is not overly concerned with what is officially religious and what is not. A cathedral should challenge and be challenged, supported by a vigorous appreciation for the many ways in which God reveals Himself. In such a secure faith there is room for both joy and foolishness and piety and moral weight. A cathedral embraces open-mindedness and glorious diversity.

A cathedral ministry reaches out to other urban parishes by providing a variety of services that strengthen the autonomy of local parishes by providing assistance the parishes could not afford on their own.

A congregation is maintained within the cathedral facilities as an important part of its ministry of Word and Sacrament. Yet activities by sister parishes, denominational leaders, and civic organizations also play an important part in a cathedral's ministry.

## How We Got Here

When I accepted a call to Historic Trinity in 1981, I found a congregation of about 50 members with a median age of 85. Today, Historic Trinity has 1,200 members, and the median age is 36.

In 1981, I was also a full-time council member of the City of Detroit and president of the Michigan League of Cities. These positions provided the opportunity to visit most major cities in the United States.

As I traveled, I noticed there was a unique aspect to downtown churches—the old St. Mary's, the First Lutheran, the Christ Episcopal. These parishes were more than private clubs, serving only card-carrying members. They were metropolitan in outreach and oriented to serving the total community. They were cross-cultural. Their facilities were used by more than the local congregation. Most of these parishes were also traditional in worship style.

Because of those observations, I determined to find a role for downtown churches in America. As part of my ministry at Historic Trinity, I established a task force comprised of marketing and public relations people to help me define a role for—and the marketing of—downtown churches. At Trinity, we had a product that was good. We had a message that was needed. And we had an outstanding facility. But few people knew about it.

We began by developing a niche for our ministry. What were we to be? What was our unique personality? What did we have to offer that others did not have? We reviewed options that others were using: day-care centers, locations for support groups such as AA, parochial schools, renting part of the facility to other agencies. We also looked at the church-growth movement, which was the "hot" ministry at the time. As a result of our self-study, we settled on being an ecclesiastical, cultural, community facility for the metro area. We began in three areas of outreach: the arts, church history, and senior citizen work.

Why the arts? The church throughout history has fostered the arts. Given the fine architecture and artifacts of Historic Trinity, it was natural for us to support the arts in downtown Detroit. We established Trinity Arts, which sponsors concerts, plays for children, a national ecclesiastical art exhibition, needle and craft workers, seminars, and organ recitals.

We also focused on our library. Our Dau Church History Library, located on the third floor of Historic Trinity, is gathering the history of all Detroit churches (past and present) of all denominations. In carrying out its mission, the Dau Library has become a national resource.

Our work with senior citizens provided a natural avenue for outreach too. In our immediate neighborhood there are 17 senior-citizen high-rise buildings. We bring one-on-one ministry to the residents of these buildings. We also provide field trips for the residents as well as monthly luncheons at Historic Trinity.

Our church building itself is an asset. Designed by the "St. James Society" (Dr. Pipekorn, Dr. Kretzmann, Dr. Webber, and Dr. Otte—familiar names in Lutheran circles), it offers the finest in liturgical architecture and lends itself to a traditional style of worship. As part of our effort to reach out to the community, we changed our name from Trinity Lutheran Church to Historic Trinity Lutheran Church and developed a logo in German script.

Today we use this logo on every letter, envelope, flyer, or program we mail or produce. When people see this logo, they immediately associate it with us. They do not have to ask, "Who is this?"

We also regularly market Historic Trinity through billboards, direct mail to targeted groups, or mass mailings to downtown residents. Regular news releases provide us with excellent exposure in the daily and community papers, on radio programs, and on TV newscasts.

It is not unusual to see a TV news team at a service or event at Historic Trinity. We have an extensive Sunday bulletin that lists all activities, a monthly newsletter mailed to the parish membership, and another newsletter, the *Messenger*, that we mail three times a year to a master list of 15,000 who have visited or contributed to the ministries of Historic Trinity.

As our new identity as the "Cathedral Church" developed, we became more than ever the gathering place and resource for Lutherans throughout metropolitan Detroit. When others said, "Lutherans do not have cathedrals," we said, "Why not?"

Thus, with the approval of the LCMS Michigan District Board of Directors, we became the Lutheran Cathedral Ministry for Detroit. Recently, the position of president emeritus of the District has been established at Historic Trinity to define a role for former district presidents throughout The Lutheran Church—Missouri Synod.

In every city, in the downtown or midtown, a church can become a cathedral ministries church. Any church can be a parish, but usually in each city only one can become the "Cathedral"—the resource and gathering place for the denomination. This cathedral ministry role ensures that the congregation will be around for many years.

As a result of our cathedral outreach, Historic Trinity has developed many "side door" ministries that bring people to our church and its facilities. We put 90,000 people through our facilities in a year, and we have an active mailing list of 15,000, as already noted. We have many visitors for all our services and provide numerous opportunities for worship.

All this is not always easy. It takes people and money to be successful. If you have a fine building and no people, you have a museum. If you have a fine building and people, but no money, you can only dream. To make a vision a reality, it takes people and money. It also requires taking risks, trying all sorts of activities, programs, and outreach ministries. The funding for Historic Trinity comes from the parish and from Historic Trinity, Inc., a nonprofit corporation that helps us with leadership issues, task forces, advice, and funding.

What are the benefits? Historic Trinity is the fastest-growing church in downtown Detroit. Today, when you think of a church in the city, you automatically think Historic Trinity. When the press is looking for a source to quote, they think, "Historic Trinity"! When people seek information on church art or church history, they think, "Historic Trinity." For special religious days such as Christmas, Good Friday, or Easter, people think, "Historic Trinity" (usually SRO—"standing room only"—at our worship services). When Lutherans seek a church to visit that conducts services like the parishes they used to attend, they think, "Historic Trinity."

Want to learn more about Historic Trinity or talk about "marketing" your parish in urban America? We invite you to visit Historic Trinity and see firsthand a dynamic downtown church in action. In some rare cases, we will visit you when there is a substantial group interested in discussing ways to begin this process.

## What We Offer as a Cathedral Church

Historic Trinity is a source of beauty and pride for all of Detroit and for all Michigan Lutherans. It is at once outrageous and orthodox, utopian and savvy, a place that overwhelms you, all at once, in a great rush of contradiction and paradox. As with any cathedral, it is a place of holy awe.

As important as these attributes are, the soul of Historic Trinity consists not in the church's physical appearance or its ecclesiastical attributes, but in our ministry. Historic Trinity is more than a social club or architectural treasure. Our ministry has at its core a vital, committed parish membership nurtured by a long tradition of solid pastoral care. Historic Trinity belongs to more than its members. It belongs to all Lutherans, who are encouraged to claim it as their own, to return to it at any time, and to bring their children to it to learn about their roots.

We also find a purpose in reaching out to the unchurched. We reach out beyond the walls of our building, beyond the lines that mark the boundaries of our property. We, like all cathedral ministries past and present, serve a far wider sphere of people than those on our membership roster. That ministry is our privilege and our responsibility.

Dr. David Eberhard has been involved in urban ministry for four decades. In addition to serving as the pastor of several Detroit churches, he was a member of the Detroit City Council from 1969 to 1993. As a religious and civic leader, he has served on many boards and commissions, including those of several national organizations. He has appeared in the pages of *Life* magazine and made numerous guest appearances on national TV. Part of Dr. Eberhard's mission at Historic Trinity Lutheran Church has been to develop a meaningful paradigm for the downtown church in America. If you are interested in cathedral ministries, Dr. Eberhard and Historic Trinity can be reached at www.historictrinity.org.

# Faith Comes by Hearing

*Spreading the Seed of the Gospel
through Video and Cable TV*

*Mark Schulz*

If "faith comes from hearing the message," how do you reach those who do not want to hear, especially if the message of the Gospel is such anathema to them that they avoid all contact with Christians?

Interesting question, isn't it? And a familiar one too. This question is especially relevant if you live and work in a university environment.

At St. Luke Lutheran Church, Ann Arbor, Mich., we believe one viable way to plant the seed of the Gospel is through video outreach on community-access cable TV. To make that method productive and effective, we have included a video studio in the plans for our new church building.

To be precise, the new studio is more of a media center. It houses facilities for a variety of electronic media, but video production, both for ourselves and perhaps for other congregations and church entities, will form the bulk of the studio's work initially.

We incorporated plans for the media center into our new building project after seven years of producing commercials and Christian-oriented programs for our local community-access channel.

You might be surprised at the number of people who watch local cable TV programming and at the impact carefully packaged Christian programming can make. We have been pleasantly surprised ourselves, and we have received many favorable comments over the years.

The key is to plant the seed of the Gospel in people's hearts. To do this, you have to produce a good product, which we have sought to do from the beginning of our efforts. (We are blessed with a number of very talented people in our congregation.)

Ann Arbor is the home of the University of Michigan. As a major college town, Ann Arbor is cosmopolitan in its outlook and diverse in its makeup.

St. Luke has been part of the community for nearly a half century. We began as an outgrowth of The Lutheran Church—Missouri Synod's campus ministry at the University of Michigan. Instead of seeking out an established church, the founders of St. Luke decided to start their own congregation. "We won't be like other Lutheran churches," they said. "We'll try new things; we'll stay fresh and cutting edge." That is not a word-for-word quote, but it gives the flavor of the goals of our founding members.

As a "cutting edge" congregation, St. Luke always has been known as the "other" Lutheran church in town. It has been the alternative. Not only did this make St. Luke attractive to Lutherans moving here who wanted something a bit different from the church of their childhood, but it also made St. Luke effective in reaching out to those not previously Lutheran.

## Harvest Fields in Michigan

Ann Arbor today is a vibrant, growing community. Over the last generation or two, many Michigan graduates have remained in the Ann Arbor area. They have accepted jobs with the university or its renowned University Hospital, opened their own businesses, or joined the staffs of business or professional organizations that have moved here to serve Ann Arbor's growing population. This expanding business and professional base has resulted in a mix of community influences different from that of the "typical" college town of a generation or two ago.

One thing that hasn't changed over the years is the determined adherence of many of Ann Arbor's opinion makers to liberal politics and liberal social agendas. This provides an ongoing challenge for Bible-believing congregations such as St. Luke. In the eyes of many, we have an unpopular message that is unwelcome in some quarters of the community. That our message is not diluted by the social gospel makes us stick out even more.

As a college town with a growing business sector, it is not uncommon to see "suits" sitting at a deli table next to a group of young adults in grunge attire, both perhaps holding to a common political/social agenda. The Lord has not gone without voice in these disparate communities, however. In and around Ann Arbor and the university there have been significant ongoing outreach efforts in the form of campus churches (denominationally based) and evangelistic groups. The Lord has used these ministries to transform the lives and eternal destinies of many a professor, nonconforming radical, and three-piece "suit."

While our larger community has experienced many changes during the past few decades, St. Luke isn't that much different from what it was 45 years ago—if one remembers the original goal: to be different and to experiment. However, to look at St. Luke today, it appears much different. We are a church that strategically chooses to offer "choices." For example, we offer three different styles of worship each weekend. We offer three different services on Christmas Eve and a different one again on Christmas Day. We have more than 100 different ministries that offer a wide range of nurture and servanthood possibilities. All of these things make us look very different than the St. Luke of 45 years ago.

As noted earlier, we are in the process of building a new facility that will include a video studio. To say that we "decided to build a new worship facility" is not quite accurate. We were forced to build because we were bursting at the seams, having long ago violated the classic "80 percent is full" rule.

It isn't easy to explain why we've included the studio. It takes much more than a sound bite, but the answer shows how video can provide an excellent outreach strategy, especially in an environment in which there is strong resistance to the good news of the Gospel.

## Night Life Adventures: How We Got Started

We began our cable-TV outreach about seven years ago by making commercials. By chance, I had seen a local church commercial on cable TV. It was terrible! *We must do better in the name of Jesus,* I told myself.

We were blessed to have a video producer in the congregation, and we produced several commercials for our community-access channel. The spots focused on perceived needs and applied the Good News. The commercials were well received, and they remain a part of our outreach today.

About the same time, I became aware of Willow Creek Community Church. I took a group of laypeople to Willow Creek to check it out. When we returned to Ann Arbor, we convened a task force to brainstorm ideas for St. Luke. From the brainstorming session, we decided to pursue something different than a "seeker" service, which describes Willow Creek's outreach effort. We decided to produce a monthly "live" event, complete with audience, that would be videotaped, edited, and broadcast on public-access TV.

Thus was born "Night Life," our first foray into the world of cable-TV broadcasting. We aimed the show at hard-core unbelievers between the ages of 35 and 40.

Each edition of "Night Life" focused on a particular topic. Our hosts interviewed an "expert" or two; the Not for Profit Band played several songs; we presented a Garrison Keillor-style readers theater piece; and we shared the Gospel as it related to the theme of the show.

We staged "Night Life" at Concordia College in Ann Arbor for two years. Then we moved the whole show to St. Luke because part of the strategy of "Night Life" was to encourage members to invite their unchurched friends to the videotaping. We reasoned that moving the production to St. Luke would make it easier for our members to do this.

There were two additional reasons we moved the show. First, I had obtained a grant to purchase some equipment of our own, and I had "appropriated" an unused corner of the church basement for an editing suite. Second, we were growing weary of dragging all the newly acquired equipment to the college and back.

Unfortunately, even with the move to St. Luke, our "studio" audience did not grow appreciably. We drew from 60 to 150 people for each show. This would have been okay had we taped the show in a small, intimate room, but the capacity of our room was 450.

The staff—remember, everyone but me was a volunteer—was somewhat demoralized by all those empty seats. To address that problem, and because the main idea of "Night Life" was to make the show an outreach effort, we decided to forgo the "live" 60-minute format in favor of a studio-recorded 30-minute show.

By moving "Night Life" into a studio we were able to ensure a much higher degree of quality, make it faster paced, and thus better hold the viewers' attention. Today, it is an effective means of sowing Gospel seeds in the lives of people who go out of their way to avoid Christians.

# New Projects, a New Building, and a New Studio

We continued to acquire equipment—a small percentage from the church budget and most of it through a donor. Meanwhile, we began to videotape worship services, edit them, and put them on cable-access TV. Then we developed an additional program that is still in the prototype phase. "Take Two" features a group of friends gathered around a table. At the table they enjoy one another's company and rehash the previous Sunday's sermon. The show is aimed at dechurched Christians, and our goal is to show viewers that "church" can be meaningful for them today.

Our video production experience has benefited St. Luke in other ways. When we realized the need to initiate a building project two years ago, we produced our own video promotion piece instead of outsourcing it, which would have cost between $13,000 and $22,000. The promo was highly successful, and last year, when it came time for the fund-raiser for our current sanctuary expansion, we produced a second video promotion piece.

When the expansion project is complete, we hope to continue all of the projects listed above, but we've also made a commitment to something new and exciting that involves the media center.

In the new sanctuary, we are installing a video screen on the wall above and behind the altar. It will be framed out and won't appear to be a screen when not in use. We are going to involve visual media in our new space.

Our rationale is simple: Beginning with the late Baby Boomers and continuing with the Busters and now the "Millennial Generation," people are increasingly visual learners. We are committed to bringing the message of God's Word in the "language of the people." Today that language is increasingly visual.

Finally, we also will record music in the new studio. We also may undertake projects for other churches at a cost much lower than they would obtain at a commercial studio. Such projects might include commercials, video lessons, and building campaign promotions. The goal of all this is to communicate the Gospel to those who are in Christ, who are seeking Christ in our midst, and those whom the Lord is seeking in our community.

I am the first to say that word of mouth is *always* the very best means of communicating the Gospel. If this is true, why pursue these other means of communication? Because those who resist God avoid Christians. Why would they want to be in the company of someone who stands for everything they don't? If faith comes by hearing the message of Christ, where will they hear the message? Ah, the beauty of TV or radio. It can bring a seed of the Gospel into their lives before they're even aware of it. The simple word of the Gospel changed Matthew's life. It changed Zacchaeus' life and Saul's life too. Today, through the medium of video, that Word can change the lives of our fellow citizens as well.

## Getting Started

By now you may be thinking, *All this is great, but how do I get started?* I suggest the following simple strategy: Pray. Read. Go. Try. Revamp. Ask.

- **Pray.** Pray for the Lord's guidance, help, creativity, and blessing.

- **Read.** Read about it. An excellent current resource is *The Media Reformation* by Michael Slaughter (Abingdon Press).

- **Go.** Attend seminars about how people think. Go to seminars on using media for outreach and worship.

- **Try.** Start small. Think big. Try small, approachable projects. Strive for quality while not biting off more than you can chew. Then strive for the larger dream.

- **Revamp.** You always will learn new and better ways of using media for inreach and outreach. Don't be afraid to revamp, grow, and change.

- **Ask.** Don't be afraid to share your unique vision of what could be with others. Don't be afraid to ask for funding: from your congregation, from like-minded people, from grant-giving organizations that value creativity in outreach.

Rev. Mark Schulz has served St. Luke Lutheran Church for eight years. His title is Minister of Worship and Creative Outreach. Rev. Schulz has a passion for leading people in worship and for reaching people with the Good News through every means God in His creativity provides.

# How to Build a Congregational Web Site

*Keven D. Ficken*

One of the most dramatic advances of this present age is the introduction of the Internet. It has had a profound impact on modern society, and many organizations, churches included, are thinking seriously about creating their own Internet sites. This chapter will provide a brief introduction to the process of establishing a Web presence for your congregation.

When considering whether your congregation should have a Web site, the very first question to answer is: *What will be the purpose of our site?*

Deciding, up front, on the focus and mission of your Web site will help you to produce a more informative and well-designed site than if you simply throw a bunch of information together and post it on a web page. It's also essential that you decide on the audience. Is the site mainly for non-Christians? prospective members? existing members? all of the above? You may even want to develop a mission statement for your congregational Web site. A mission statement will provide you with a constant reminder of your site's purpose and serve as a guide for deciding whether future content is suitable.

Once your congregation has decided to produce a Web site and has decided on the purpose of that site, there are two main areas that need to be addressed before your site is ready to go online. First, you need to find a place to host your Web pages. Second, you need to find someone to produce and maintain the content.

# Hosting the Site

There are a variety of options when it comes to hosting your Web site. The most inexpensive way to host a Web site is to use a free Web site-hosting service. These services provide a small amount of disk space to individuals or organizations seeking a place to host a Web site. The majority of these sites provide free space because they make money through advertising. Generally, if your Web site is hosted through one of these providers, you will find advertisements either within your page or within a separate advertisement window that opens when your page is loaded.

A downside to using one of these services is the long, often complicated Web address (or URL) that people will need to use to access your site. Also, the amount of disk space provided by the service might not be enough for those who want to provide large amounts of information on their site.

Service and support are two additional issues to keep in mind with one of these free services. There may not be easy access to someone who can help with questions or problems. Often, the use of scripting or other more advanced techniques is not permitted on these sites either.

While there are a number of limitations to using a free Web space provider, congregations who have limited resources or who are interested in testing a site with minimal investment may find these services provide a valuable option.

The other principal option for Web hosting is to use a commercial Internet service provider (or ISP). These companies are in the business of hosting web sites and providing access to the Internet for a fee. There are a vast number of national and local ISPs from which to choose. Generally, an account with one of these companies will include access to the Web and the rest of the Internet, one or more e-mail accounts, and a certain amount of server space for hosting a Web site. The fee for such services usually runs about $20 per month.

If there will be a need to access your account from different parts of the country, then a national ISP is a good choice. In most major cities, national ISPs usually have local phone numbers from which you can dial into your account. However, if there is no need for this, a local ISP might be the better route to take. You often will get better service and more personal support from a local service provider. Most people who have access to the Internet already have disk space for Web hosting allotted to them through their provider—they just may not know it.

A third option that may be available to some is free hosting through another organization. If your congregation is associated with a local university, a national church body, or some other institution, you might have access to Web server space through that organization. Likewise, if someone in your congregation works for a company that provides Web space for employees, this individual may be willing to use some of his or her space for the congregational Web site. In any case, it definitely pays to check for any connections that someone in the congregation may have before paying for an account with an ISP.

## Producing the Web Site

Once you have found a place to host your site, you need to find someone to create and maintain it. It's important to identify a contact person in the congregation who will take the lead and be responsible for the Web site. This person does not necessarily have to be the individual who actually produces the content (though it helps). He or she does need to take control of what information gets posted on the site. This helps to insure that information remains current and that the information on the site is not objectionable or inappropriate.

Once this person has been identified, you can find someone to produce the pages. Many congregations have members who have created Web pages. It might be a good idea to run a notice in the church bulletin or newsletter, asking for volunteers. Don't forget to ask your youth group. Most kids are attuned to the Web, and many have their own Web sites. This is a great opportunity to get your youth more involved in the church.

If there is no one in the congregation who is willing or able to produce your Web content, then you can hire a consultant (which can get expensive) or learn to do it yourself. Believe it or not, creating a Web page is not that difficult. There are many tools available that make this task simple.

If you decide to learn how to create the Web site yourself, you first need to learn a little about HTML (Hypertext Mark-up Language), which is the language of the Web. There are dozens of books available from any good bookstore that will teach you the basics of HTML. There also are a number of Web sites that offer HTML tutorials.

The beauty of HTML is that it is a mark-up language and not a programming language. This means the creation of a Web page simply involves the insertion of specific "tags" into a text file. These tags cause the text of the document to be aligned and displayed in certain ways. Once you have learned what some of the simple tags are and how they work, it's easy to produce a simple Web page. In fact, you can look at the source code for any Web page on the Internet by selecting "View Source" in your Web browsing software (such as Netscape Navigator or Microsoft Internet Explorer). This will allow you to see how others have created their pages.

There are also software packages available to help you create your Web page. These programs are usually referred to as HTML editors. Some programs provide menus or buttons for specific HTML tags. You simply click on these tags to insert them into your document. There are also programs available that do not require the user to know or even view the HTML source code. These programs, often referred to as WYSIWYG editors (pronounced "wizzy-wig," which stands for "What You See Is What You Get"), work just like desktop-publishing or word-processing software. With this type of software, you can drag and drop text and images and use the mouse to control the appearance and alignment of the page.

Of course, an HTML editor is not necessary for producing a Web page. Any text editor such as Notepad, Wordpad, or Simpletext can be used to create a Web page. By typing in the desired text, typing in the HTML tags, and saving the document with an ".htm" or ".html" extension, you can easily produce a Web page with any text editor. Also, many recent versions of the major word-processing programs allow you to convert your word-processed document to an HTML file. These utilities do not always produce the most elegant-looking Web pages, but they are better than nothing.

Once your Web site has been created, your ISP can provide you with software and information about how to upload your site to the Web. After this has happened, your site is online and ready to be viewed. The only task left is to publicize the site with all of the major Web indices and search engines so people can find your site. Often, if you are part of a large organization or institution, that organization or institution may help you do this as well.

## Resources for Web Page Creators

Here is a list of resources that may help get you started. The following does not constitute an endorsement of these resources but is offered as an example of what is available, based on comments from churches, other religious organizations, and respected Web page developers. Although these resources were current at the publication of this booklet, they may or may not be current when you read this material. That is also the nature of the Internet and the World Wide Web. Change is constant.

## Free Internet Service Providers (ISPs)

- **Geocities** <http://www.geocities.com>—You get a free Web page with 11 megabytes of space for your site, Web development tools, and technical support.

- **Houses of Worship** <http://www.housesofworship.net>— Claims to have an editable Web page on their site for every church in North America. Log on and see if your church is there.

- **Luther95.org** <http://www.luther95.org/>—This organization provides up to five megabytes of free Web server space to Lutheran churches.

- **Net Ministries** <http://netministries.org>—Net Ministries is a nonprofit corporation providing a free Internet presence to qualifying Christian charitable organizations, ministries, and churches.

## HTML Tutorials

- **A Beginner's Guide to HTML** <http://www.ncsa.uiuc.edu/General/Internet/WWW/HTMLPrimer.html>—A great place to start for information on HTML.

- **Developer Shed** <http://www.devshed.com>—"A resource to build a better Web site." Provides tools, tutorials, and discussion on a variety of Web development topics.

- **So you want to make a Web Page!** <http://junior.apk.net/~jbarta/tutor/makapage/>—Another good HTML tutorial for beginners.

- **The bare bones guide to HTML** <http://werbach.com/barebones/>—Yet another HTML primer.

- **Very Basic Help With Images**
  <http://www.aphids.com/susan/imhelp/>—A good resource for learning about the use and placement of inline graphics in your page.

## Software

- **Netscape Communicator and Composer**
  <http://www.netscape.com>—Free Web browser and graphical HTML editor.

- **Microsoft Internet Explorer and FrontPage**
  <http://www.microsoft.com>—Microsoft's Web browser and HTML editor. Internet Explorer is free, but FrontPage is not.

- **Bbedit** <http://www.barebones.com>—A good text-based HTML editor for the Macintosh. This is a commercial product, but there is also a free "lite" version of the software.

- **Webber32** <http://www.webber32.com>—A good text-based HTML editor for Windows. This is also a commercial product. A trial version can be downloaded for free.

- **TUCOWS** <http://www.tucows.com>—This site is a great place to learn about and download a variety of Web-related software. Programs are rated and described.

## Graphics

- **Animated Christian Graphics** <http://www.inspired-tech.com/gallery.htm>—A collection of animated graphics with a Christian theme.

- **Christian Images Gallery**
  <http://www.christianmedia.co.uk/gallery/menu.htm>—This site contains regular and animated graphics.

- **The Icon Bank** <http://www.iconbank.com>—A searchable image archive.

- **Religious Icon and Image Archive**
  <http://www.aphids.com/susan/relimage/>—A collection of graphics with Christian themes.

### Discussions

- **LCMS-WEB**—An e-mail listserv, this forum provides an opportunity for LCMS Web developers to discuss problems and share information. To subscribe, send an e-mail message to mailserv@crf.cuis.edu and in the body of the message, not the subject line, type the words SUBSCRIBE LCMS-WEB. You should receive a confirmation within 15 minutes.

- **USENET**—There are a variety of Usenet groups devoted to Internet and Web-related topics. Ask your ISP for information on accessing Usenet Newsgroups.

### Other Resources

- **LiveUpdate** <http://www.liveupdate.com>—Creators of the Crescendo streaming MIDI music player.

- **Map Blast** <http://www.mapblast.com>—This site provides maps of any address or location in the United States or Canada.

- **MapQuest** <http://www.mapquest.com>—Contains customizable maps of any location in the world and driving directions to any destination in the United States.

- **RealNetworks** <http://www.real.com>—The makers of the Real Media Player and Server, which enable one to play or send streaming audio and video over the Internet.

- **SuperStats** <http://www.superstats.com>—Provides free Web site statistics for your site.

  Keven D. Ficken is Electronic Media Specialist for The Lutheran Church—Missouri Synod. He is responsible for maintaining the LCMS Web presence and developing Web content. This chapter is adapted from his presentation "Building a Congregational Web Site" on the LCMS Web page and is used by permission. Ficken is a graduate of Concordia University, Irvine, Calif.

# Let Your Sign Shine!

*Ronald Glusenkamp*

In his dialog with God, the Old Testament prophet Habakkuk complains bitterly about the state of affairs in his world. There is violence, wrongdoing, problems, and pain. (Sound familiar?) The people of God suffer at the hands of the Babylonians. Habakkuk asks what God's plan is, and God states: "Write the vision, make it plain on tablets, so that a runner may read it" (2:2 NRSV).

Those words can inspire and guide a church-sign ministry that can enlighten and entertain. God's command to Habakkuk can offer new opportunities to share the Good News in your community.

Communications specialists estimate that we are bombarded each day with 16,000 messages. These messages are everywhere: television, radio, newspapers, cell phones, faxes, and e-mail, to name just a few. And how many of those messages enlighten and entertain?

Unfortunately, the answer is very few. By creatively using your outdoor church sign, you can "write the vision" so runners, walkers, bicyclists, and motorists can read it.

## The Church with the Sign

Your congregation probably has a sign in front of its building. Most likely, the potential of this sign is not being maximized. What's even worse, it might be communicating something negative about God or your congregation.

The intent of this chapter is to inspire, explain, and be a resource for how an ordinary aspect of your church property can become an extraordinary 24-hour-a-day witness to the Gospel. Your sign can be an evangelism tool for making your congregation known in your community and for connecting faith life with daily happenings.

People are thirsty for the refreshing good news of Jesus. However, sometimes individuals and congregations are guilty of "promoting thirst without quenching it," a criticism leveled by one contemporary author. What an indictment! It ought to move us to spring into action to meet the needs of those who hunger and thirst for the Living Water.

Not too long after I arrived at Gethsemane, someone asked, "What do you think you want up on the marquee?" *Marquee?* The word struck me because it didn't sound very church oriented. I almost corrected the questioner because his choice of words sounded too much like show business. But the more I thought about it, the more I realized a "marquee" is exactly what a church sign can be.

A dictionary defines *marquee* as (1) a large tent with open sides, used chiefly for outdoor entertainment; (2) a rooflike structure, often bearing a signboard, projecting over an entrance, as to a theater or hotel; (3) a star performer, someone or something people go out of their way to see.

I like the idea of having a big tent (it sounds very biblical to me). However, we don't have a tent, just a sign that we use to convey information in a humorous manner.

Gethsemane is located at the corner of a busy intersection. I want people to drive by (or walk or jog or ride by) and at first laugh or chuckle but then think about what our sign says.

Our sign is a popular topic of conversation. One message appeared in the *National Enquirer.* Others have appeared in the *American Banker,* the *Orange Country Register,* the *St. Louis Post-Dispatch,* and the *South Side Journal.* Recently, there have been news stories on the sign itself. Radio talk-show hosts comment on the sign during drive time. (It's important to note that while we are known as "the church with the sign," we are not "the sign with the church.")

In the end, of course, all this "sign talk" is really about stewardship, using a gift that has been given. The sign at Gethsemane was there when I arrived. It had the usual boring information on it: times of services, the pastor's name, the identification of our denomination. From time to time the sign was changed (I am told it was done on an annual basis), but there wasn't a plan or even an appreciation for the effect we could have with the sign. In fact, it didn't really enter much into the thinking of our evangelism program at all.

All that changed one day when I wrote a sign about Roseanne Barr. It was right after she "sang" the national anthem. The sign appeared in the fall, the very time congregations typically recruit choir members. I put up the following words:

*Roseanne Barr doesn't*
*sing here*
*but you can!*

Lots of people took note, and the response was a chorus of positive comments. People talked about the sign. And not just members, but folks who drove past the church. They would call the secretary or tell me they went out of their way to see what was on the sign. The more feedback I received, the more I thought about the sign as a way to enlighten and entertain people.

## Some Sign Basics

If you are in the market for a church sign, here are some things to consider.

Visit with representatives from local sign companies. There are two basic types of signs: single face and double face. Normally, it isn't good to be "double faced," but I suggest you make an exception when it comes to selecting your church sign. A single-face sign is appropriate if traffic comes from one direction only or if the placement of the sign requires only a single face. A double-face sign gives you more options (for example, two different messages at the same time) with a higher potential to make impressions.

The most popular size for a church sign is 4 feet by 8 feet. While this sign would look large in the living room of the parsonage or in the sacristy, it is an appropriate outdoor size. It can be set up with a "post" mount, which is normally included in the price of the sign, or with a "base mount," which may include a pedestal of brick or stone (normally an extra-cost item).

The standard size for church sign letters is 4 or 6 inches. Remember, size does matter! The larger the letter, the more striking and bold the image. Letters are usually black, but some suppliers carry them in red, blue, and green too. I use black letters exclusively because I try to make my words and messages colorful. However, you might want to experiment with different colors during the seasons of the church year.

## Some Things to Avoid

An effective church sign resembles a conversation between friends. The discourse is based on mutual respect and admiration. The tone of the conversation is casual; it doesn't SHOUT, SCREAM, YELL, or HOLLER! Statements that appear to be ultimatums or threats don't have a place in such a dialog. As a Christian who dearly loves the church, it pains me to say that I'm often offended by the messages I read on church signs. The offense is not based on the scandal of the crucified Christ (1 Corinthians 1:22–23) but appears to be generated from an unkind spirit. In some ways it comes across as "We have it and you don't, too bad!"

One often-seen church sign reads:

*No Jesus—No peace*

*Know Jesus—Know peace!*

While Christians believe and teach that because of Jesus there is a "peace of God, which transcends all understanding" (Philippians 4:7), I maintain that this message offers little "peace" or "understanding." Messages should offer joyful "insight," not a woeful call to "incite." We want to share God's peace, not tear someone to pieces.

Another sign I often see during Lent reads:

*If Christianity were a crime,*
*Would there be enough evidence*
*To convict you?*

Obviously, the intention is to make you feel guilty that you haven't committed enough "crimes" to warrant an arrest. My hunch is that the person who doesn't know Jesus will not understand the nuance. Or they simply may plead no contest. And it's likely that those who do know Jesus will either feel "cross" that the church is judging them or despair about their own faith journey.

It has been my experience that the signs that connect reflect a sense of humor and a feeling of empathy. Isaiah was called by God to "comfort, comfort, My people, … speak tenderly to Jerusalem, and proclaim to her that her hard service has been completed, that her sin has been paid for, that she has received from the LORD's hand double for all her sins" (Isaiah 40:1–2). In a world that is inhospitable to people who try to walk in the footsteps of our Savior, how significant it is to be a place that promotes God's soothing words of comfort and welcome.

I also see lots of signs that don't reflect the joy of the Gospel. Instead, they are legalistic, negative, and judgmental. Words such as *should, ought,* and *must* regularly appear alongside words (and serious realities) such as *sin, death,* and *hell.* At times, too, the rhetoric on these signs is of the "insider" variety. One would have to be well versed in church history to "get it."

On the other hand, one need not be shy about stating quite bold-ly "who we are and Whose we are." The church sign is different from the sign for the local bank or service station. It is appropriate and even commanded that Christians let their light shine before others.

## Things to Do

Your sign is a snapshot of who you are and what your church believes about God, how it feels about the major issues of the day, and what your sense is regarding the times in which we live. It's a challenge to say something faithful, humorous, and inviting in just five to seven medium-sized words. Yet that's part of the fun. Here are some things to consider when creating messages for your sign.

- Make sure there is plenty of LIGHT and LITE in the picture.
- Focus on the POSITIVES.
- Direct attention to the WORD.
- FLASH—make it timely.
- Expose the VALUES and BENEFITS of being loved by God.
- Try it from several different ANGLES.
- Leave it to the tabloids or someone else to develop the NEG-ATIVES!

### Public Service Announcements

Christians are in the world but not of the world. Congregations, when asked what their mission is, often will answer with the words of Matthew 28:19–20. However, having made that profession, which has global implications, the same congregation will behave as if it isn't a member of the community in which it exists. When the president of the neighborhood association asks that a notice be posted on the church sign regarding a community rummage sale (the proceeds of which will benefit an after-school latchkey program), the response is a curt no. Or worse, it's a long negative answer filled with complaints and accusations about neighborhood dogs that fertilize the flowers in the churchyard.

A church sign can be a bridge to your community or it can be a wall. By posting public service announcements, you can accomplish several things: First, you say, "We care about this community." Second, you say, "We care about something besides ourselves." When we care for others, we are doing what Jesus called us to do. Matthew 25 is a wonderful testimony to the call to have "evangelical eyes," to see Jesus in the people whom we serve.

Public service announcements are just that, *service.* They announce an event that serves the public. When the St. Louis Public Library celebrated its centennial recently, I posted the following on our sign:

*Bibliophiles have*
*100s of smiles*
*The Library is 100!*

When the library was promoting a registration drive, this sign made a great deal of sense:

*The card to access*
*The card of success*
*A library card—check it out!*

Our friends at the library were thrilled that we recognized and celebrated their birthday and promoted an important campaign.

The Bible provides wonderful guidelines for creating messages. I like to refer to our messages as "drive-by sermons." Stated simply, build up, don't tear down. Be invitational, not judgmental. Include, don't exclude.

Your church sign can be a major component in your evangelism program. It lets people know that you are thinking of them and, more important, that God loves them.

Our congregation sponsors an ice-cream social every year. The Sunday following the event we state:

*Nothing is sweeter*
*Than one of our*
*Sundays!*

Rev. Ronald Glusenkamp is pastor of Gethsemane Lutheran Church, St. Louis, Mo. This chapter is based on his book *Signs for These Times* (Concordia, 1998). Rev. Glusenkamp is recognized as a leader in using the media to tell a congregation's story. News stories about Gethsemane have appeared on television, in newspapers, and on radio. Rev. Glusenkamp has previously served parishes in Kansas City, Mo., and Wichita, Kans.